ART DECO FASHION

GEORGE BARBIER 1921

ART DECO FASHION
FRENCH DESIGNERS 1908-1925

MARTIN BATTERSBY

ACADEMY EDITIONS · LONDON / ST. MARTIN'S PRESS · NEW YORK

Published in the United States of America by
St. Martin's Press 175 Fifth Avenue New York NY 10010

Library of Congress Catalog Card Number 74-81477
ISBN 0-312-05181-6 (USA only)

Published in Great Britain by
Academy Editions 7 Holland Street London W8

Printed in Shen Zhen, China.

Frontispiece
George Barbier La Belle Dame Sans
Merci, robe du soir, de Worth, 1921.

IN no other country has fashion been taken so seriously as in France. For many generations Paris was the artistic centre of France, the magnet attracting talent from the rest of the country and often from abroad. So the supremacy of Paris at the turn of the century in one of the most important branches of the decorative arts was a matter of pride to be jealously guarded and upheld. The rest of the western world looked to Paris as a source of new fashions and new variations on old themes. Nowhere else could be found such a concentration of talents dedicated to the enhancement of the female sex, of artists who could apply their fastidious skills to the creation of a dress 'embodying a harmony and rhythm of line and colour'—a work of art in every detail of design and craftsmanship. An ensemble from one of the great couturiers was a reflection of the spirit of the time and as changes in thoughts and attitudes occurred they found an echo in fashion. Added to this was an element of fantasy often bordering on the perverse by means of which the humdrum realities of everyday life were transformed and enlivened.

Above all, the quality in which Parisian designers excelled with such apparent ease and which so often eluded designers from other countries was that of elegance. Indefinable but immediately recognisable by the initiated, it is not to be confused with chic, with its implications of a certain noticeable smartness. Elegance is indefinable simply because there are no hard and fast rules by which it can be achieved and in itself can be a matter of contradictions. It can be exaggeration or restraint, excess or elimination and can shift from one extreme to the other with no apparent reason. Physical attributes are, on the whole, of rather less importance than a certain mental attitude and a dress which is the epitome of elegance on one woman will appear dowdy or even ostentatious on another. Neither is wealth a necessary factor in achieving elegance for although an extremely rich woman has obviously a far wider choice and can enlist the aid of the best talents in her clothes and surroundings, one less affluent can create a greater effect of elegance by simpler means.

Quite apart from the artistic prestige which the dictatorship of fashion conferred on Paris another consideration was of very great importance. Fashion played a preponderant role in the economy of France. In 1924, for instance, the export of women's clothing—and this excluded the duty-free models sold by the couture houses to foreigners—amounted to the enormous sum of two and a half thousand million francs. To this could be added the revenue from millinery,

1 Paul Iribe *Les Robes de Paul Poiret,* 1908.

2 Pául Iribe *Les Robes de Paul Poiret,* 1908.

bags, stockings and furs—the export of the humble rabbit skins treated to imitate more costly furs brought in another two hundred and fifty million francs alone. The increasing use of cosmetics in the 'twenties together with a widening range of scents was another profitable source; perfume alone was exported to the value of six hundred and fifty million francs compared to a pre-war revenue of sixty millions. Lingerie of silk or artificial silk accounted for four hundred millions while artificial flowers and feathers still another one hundred millions.

Not all these vast sums came from the export of luxury items, of course, but it was the luxury items which provided the prestige and helped to sell the less expensive products. The number of women able to devote the time, care and money to being entirely dressed and otherwise enhanced by the leading Parisian couturiers was minute in comparison with the vast buying public outside France. But it was they, constantly photographed, who brought to the attention of the less affluent the desirability of anything bearing a French label. Even a pair of gloves from the rue Royale could hopefully give their wearer something of Parisian style even if the rest of her wardrobe came from the local dressmaker.

Thus the leading fashion houses with their highly expert staffs of cutters, fitters, *vendeuses* and models played an important role in French life for upon their imagination and flair depended the livelihoods of innumerable manufacturers of silk and woollen fabrics, buttons, leatherwork, ribbons and so on—even the glass workers, making their exquisite bottles for perfumes. Clients —women of natural or acquired elegance—were of equal importance, for it was upon their

4 Paul Iribe *Les Robes de Paul Poiret,* 1908.

5 Paul Méras Advertisement for 'High-Life Tailor', 1910.

Quelle Fleur

POURRAIT VOUS ÊTRE COMPARÉE?

6 Paul Iribe Advertisement for Bichara ('Parfumeur Syrien'), Paris, 1912. Bichara catered for the current oriental fashions with their exotically named scents: 'Nirvana', 'Sakountala', 'Bosphora', etc. and with eye makeup named 'Mokoheul' and 'Cillana'.

approval or disdain that the collective effort of these craftsmen depended. The belief that dressmakers imposed their will upon their clients could be said to have a certain truth but certainly in the period with which this volume is concerned the reverse was more likely to be the case. Princess Bibesco, author of *Noblesse de Robe*, describes the reactions of a discriminating Frenchwoman, given the name of Claude, to the choice of a new season's wardrobe: firstly, she chooses her clothes alone with no husband, lover or friend to influence her judgment. In this she differs from the Englishwoman who is invariably accompanied by one or more friends, the Mexican accompanied by the whole family, the Italian with her dog and *cicisbeo*, the Russian with her painter, and the Argentinian with her husband. After having carefully watched the mannequin parade undisturbed 'she leaves the church for the confessional' and in the narrow mirror-lined fitting room she looks at herself with impersonal and critical eyes for she is aware

7 Georges Lepape 'Les Jupes-Culottes', *Les Choses de Paul Poiret,* 1911. Forecast of the fashions of the future.

8 Georges Lepape *Les Choses de Paul Poiret,* 1911.

9, 10 Georges Lepape *Les Choses de Paul Poiret*, 1911.

of things about herself that no other person in the world except her fitter knows. Armed with this self knowledge she chooses. She would not even begin to make the wrong judgment of the Spanish woman in the next fitting room—a little too short in the leg and broad in the back —whom Claude can overhear being diplomatically discouraged from ordering a grey satin sheath dress by her *vendeuse* who murmurs 'I would not advise that dress for madame—it is inclined to age the hips'. Claude was in fact the archetype of a class, perhaps unique to Paris, which applied the same meticulous standards, both to their clothes and their surroundings. Rich and cultured they had an Athenian desire for novelty and surprise; Serge Diaghilev's command to Jean Cocteau, 'Astonish me', was typical of their attitude to life. A new couturier, painter, writer, poet, musician or decorative artist would be discovered, fêted and indulged —but only as long as he could provide dazzling tours-de-force of originality which satisfied

11 Paul Iribe Advertisement for linens made by La Cour Batave, 1912.

12 Paul Iribe Advertisement for 'Ilka', scent by Piver, 1912.

13 Paul Iribe Advertisement for artificial pearls made by Suclier et Cie, Paris, 1912.

the exacting standards of elegance. But were he to show the least falling off in inspiration, he was liable to be discarded with the devastating tag 'ordinaire' in favour of a newer talent. Demanding as it may have been, this patronage was the spur which kept creative talent above the level of mediocrity; in consequence a standard of design was maintained which no other European country could equal.

Traditionally there was in France less rigid distinction between the decorative and the fine arts, that is painting and sculpture. The two branches had grown apart during the nineteenth century until in England, for instance, the word 'decorative' had a rather derogatory implication; a lack of seriousness, a suggestion of amateur arty-craftiness. But in France fashion was considered one of the important decorative arts, as can be seen in the foreword to the catalogue of the International Exhibition of Decorative and Industrial Arts held in Paris in 1925. After commenting on the unchallenged supremacy of Paris in this field, the writer states that 'this superiority rightly entitles fashion to a privileged showing, for it is essentially an art'. The latest styles and models were discussed and analysed in as much detail as the work of a new painter. Just as there were more journals devoted to the decorative arts than in any other country so there were more that concentrated on fashion. This superabundance of magazines, many of high standards of printing and design, started about 1912 and coincided with the

16 Mlle. Bert Fashionable muffs and stoles. *Fémina,* 1912.

17 Mlle. Bert Afternoon dresses by Bazau. *Fémina,* 1912.

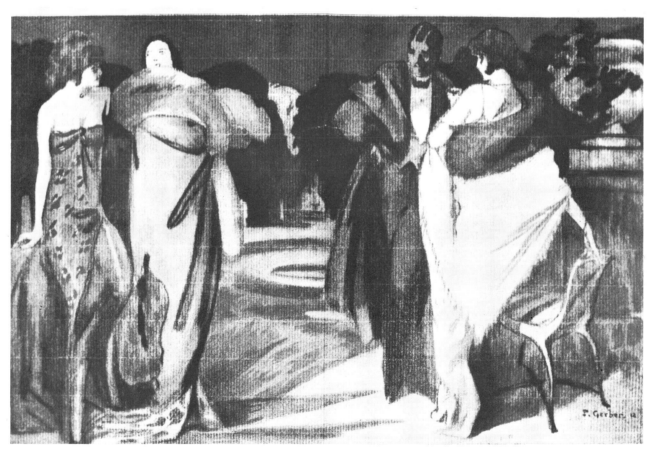

18 Pierre Gerber Evening wear by Callot Soeurs. *Comoedia Illustre,* 1912. An unusually free and impressionistic fashion illustration showing the influence of Léon Bakst and the Ballets Russes in the brilliant colouring of citron yellow, violet and cerise, later to be 'invented' in the 'thirties by Schiaparelli and called 'Shocking Pink.'

19 André Marty 'Tais-Toi, mon Coeur', *Gazette du Bon Ton,* 1913. Afternoon dress by Doeuillet of broderie anglaise and Malines lace over a sheath of black crêpe satin. Sleeves of handkerchief linen with belt and cuffs of emerald green satin.

emergence of the Art Deco style and reflected the influence of the Ballets Russes.

The reasons for this upsurge were various. Firstly, was the appearance of influential couturiers such as Paul Poiret and Jeanne Lanvin, whose talents were not confined to the designing of clothes but extended to other branches of the decorative arts; secondly it was the simultaneous coming to power of a large coterie of illustrators capable of capturing the essential spirit of contemporary fashion and creating drawings which combined an assured and distinctive draughtsmanship with wit and elegance. This particular combination is more difficult to achieve than is generally realised and the art of conveying the particular qualities of a dress by means of line and colour cannot be easily learnt. The memoirs of former editors of fashion magazines are revealing testimony to the tactful handling needed to keep the star illustrators reasonably contented and the machinations exercised to entice them from one magazine to another. An academic drawing of a model in, for instance, an evening dress can more often than not make both model and dress look dowdy and commonplace. The exact delineation of the ensemble no matter how perfectly proportioned the model or how beautiful the dress can turn out to be as uninspiring as the contemporary untouched photographs in the 'twenties magazine *Les Modes,* where the models, despite the lovely dresses from the leading couturiers which they are wearing, are noticeably lacking in distinction and in fact do a great disservice to the clothes themselves. Distortion and exaggeration have to be employed to a greater or lesser degree. Elongation of the figure is the most common device—and it can vary from dress to dress. An examination of the examples illustrated will show an interesting comparison of the different ways in which the artists carefully adapted their individual styles to depict the essential quality of each dress.

At the beginning of the sixteenth century artists began to take an interest in depicting costume and fashion as subjects in their own right. Instead of being used as trappings to enhance and underline the power and riches of the sitter in a portrait, the clothes themselves became the

focal point and the wearer an anonymous dummy serving only as a framework often exaggerated in its proportions to emphasise the characteristic line. Albrecht Dürer and Hans Holbein obviously derived great pleasure in depicting the fantastic garments worn by German and Swiss mercenaries in the first decades of the sixteenth century as did their contemporaries Peter Flötner and Daniel Hopfer in series of engravings of soldiers where every detail of their bizarre semi-uniforms which appear to have been slashed to ribbons and carefully reassembled was drawn with meticulous care. Hans Aldegraver in a series of engravings dated 1580 employed a deliberate distortion in showing the intricate voluminous clothes worn by elegant men and women by making the figures inhumanly tall with tiny heads to emphasise the bulk of their clothing—the use of a small head being a device much used subsequently.

In the sixteenth century fashion changed not only from country to country but from city to city and collections of engravings were made as records of these regional differences. Enea Vico, Jost Amman, J. J. Boissard and Theodore de Bry recorded the characteristics of various cities, Rome and Venice for instance, and in addition those of different social ranks. These artists were working during the latter years of the sixteenth century and this trend continued during the seventeenth century when the centres of fashion seem to have moved to France and to a lesser extent to England. Abraham Bosse was an indefatigable recorder of fashion in France extending his interest to relate fashion to contemporary interior decoration during the 1620's and 1630's. Wenzel Hollar concentrated on the costume of Holland and England during the pre-Cromwellian period and his drawing of a muff of fur and brocade dating from 1647 elevated a fashionable accessory into a work of art.

By the end of the seventeenth century Paris was already beginning to assert supremacy as a dictator of fashion due to the deliberate policy of Louis XIV of concentrating the political, intellectual, artistic and social life around him at Versailles. The splendour which resulted as the rich competed in displays of magnificence set the tone for the rest of Europe. Changes in

I-II René Lelong Furs designed by Revillon Frères for the winter of 1910. Left, Ermine cape and muff bordered with skunk; Right, Coat of natural sable. These drawings for the magazine *Fémina* are better examples of the conventional fashion drawings before the new influence engendered by Paul Poiret's two volumes made itself felt. The figures are of natural proportions with none of the exaggerations which would later become accepted as the norm.

III Georges Lepape   Colour plate from *Les Choses de Paul Poiret,* 1911.   The models are shown in a box at a theatre where a performance of a ballet, possibly *Cléopâtre,* is taking place and the colours of the dresses and the decor show the influence of the Ballets Russes as much as the oriental feeling in the clothes themselves.

IV Georges Lepape Colour plate from *Les Choses de Paul Poiret*, 1911. The girl's head topped by a turban with an upstanding aigrette is set against a background of a formal *parterre* garden; the mouth and eyes of the model demonstrate that Poiret considered heavy makeup a necessary accompaniment to his dresses.

V **Paul Iribe** 'Près de Vous'. Colour advertisement for the scent made by Rigaud, 1912.

21 Pierre Brissaud 'Je suis perdue . . .', *Gazette du Bon Ton,* 1913. Shantung summer dress with printed cotton muslin belt. Chéruit model.

22 Robert Dammy 'Le Coup de Vent', *Gazette du Bon Ton,* 1913. Tailormade in navy blue serge with apricot linen blouse. Jacques Doucet model.

23 Strimpl Illustration to an article by Francis de Miomandre, 'Fourrures d'hier et d'aujourd'hui', suggesting fantastic ways of using fur as a decorative accessory, *Gazette du Bon Ton,* 1913.

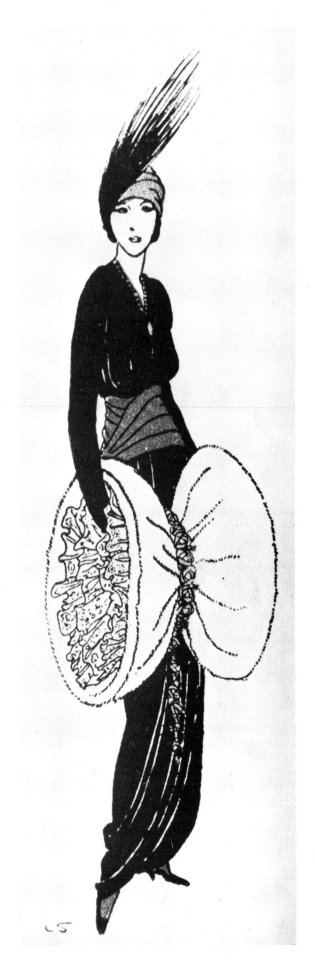

24, 25 Strimpl Illustrations to an article by Francis de Miomandre, 'Fourrures d'hier et d'aujourd'hui', suggesting fantastic ways of using fur as a decorative accessory, *Gazette du Bon Ton,* 1913.

fashion were slower at that time, partly because information about new styles took longer to disseminate and also because the clothes of the affluent classes were made by hand in richer fabrics and not discarded until worn out. The fantasies of fashion were more to be found in such accessories as fans, gloves, ruffs or the novel uses of ribbons and laces. News of changes were conveyed to other countries by fashion dolls dressed in the actual materials of the originals or by the engravings of Bonnard, and, in the eighteenth century, Gravelot and Moreau *le jeune.* The idea of a publication devoted entirely to fashion for both men and women developed in the last quarter of the eighteenth century and the *Collection des Habillements modernes et galants* dating from 1775 is one of the earliest examples. In the 1780's there appeared the *Magasin des Modes,* the *Cabinet des Modes* and the *Galerie des Modes.* Though their hand-coloured engravings are of no great artistic merit and the figures are doll-like, with exaggeratedly small waists to emphasise the current fashions, they serve their purpose in conveying the essential characteristics. Much space is devoted to hats—fantastic, ornate confections of laces, ribbons, feathers and artificial flowers—which had ousted the equally elaborate—and sometimes vermin infested—coiffures of the preceding decades.

La Mesangère flourished in Paris around 1800. It was the first magazine to show a model in a

simple but lifelike situation thus giving more interest than the usual standing figure. The opportunities for depicting draperies in motion were seized upon to create far livelier compositions than had hitherto been the case and a further interest was added by the captions. A girl in a high wind with skirts and scarves fluttering exclaims as her companion chases his beaver hat in the background 'Ah! Quel Vent!'; poised to ascend a flight of steps while her cavalier kisses her hand, she promises 'A ce soir'. In this way an attempt is made to relate fashion to everyday life or at least its more sentimental and even slightly erotic aspects. Here again there is a considerable elongation of the figures with small heads, hands and feet. When the *Gazette du Bon Ton* was founded in 1912 it was surely a deliberate attempt to recreate, captions and all, the style of *La Mesangère*.

It was at this period that the number of illustrated fashion magazines began to increase. There was the *Journal des Dames* which paid attention to men's fashions and *Le Bon Genre* which both recorded and caricatured the current styles, particularly during the Directoire when the eccentric and often grotesque fashions of the *merveilleuses* and their male equivalents gave ample scope for satire. Here too the models are shown in groups occupied in some pastime and were identified by a descriptive caption. England, too, had its share of fashion journals—the origin of most of the models displayed being French—and the *Gallery of Fashion*, Ackerman's *Repository of Art* and *La Belle Assemblée* (the use of a French name easily pronounced by an English tongue is significant of the trend to Gallic inspiration) record both male and female costume during the Regency period. Germany was served by the *Berlinischer Damenklader* and the *Hamburger Journal der Moden und Eleganz*—Hamburg had been a refuge for many aristocratic émigrés en

26 Stefano Advertisement for 'Indra' artificial pearls, 1913.

route for England and Scandinavia during the Revolution and some of the elegance of these birds of passage remained as a lingering influence. The *Weiner Mode* and the *Wiener Zeitschrift* catered for Austria. However, these noticeably lacked the stylish qualities of their French counterparts and the draughtsmanship was amateurish though with a certain charm.

As the century progressed the standard of drawing improved and the models became less stiff, posing with greater ease and grace. *La Mode,* published in the 1830's, employed Gavarni, also a contributor to the *Journal des Modes* and he must be counted among the most brilliant illustrators of fashion, crystallising in his drawings the spirit of the Romantic period when upswept hair arranged in intricate asymmetric loops entwined with flowers set off long necks and sloping shoulders rising from exaggeratedly puffed sleeves. The short, full crinolines

27 Paul Méras Dress designed by Maison Buzenet for wear at Deauville. Advertisement inserted in *Gazette du Bon Ton,* 1913.

revealed tiny feet in delicate slippers. His drawings of costumes for a *bal masqué* published in 1831 have an added quality of perverse mystery rarely found in this genre. The drawings of Etienne Drian, particularly those done in 1915 for a wartime number of *Gazette du Bon Ton,* show the influence of Gavarni in the sophisticated elegance and arrested movement of the model. It should be emphasised that these drawings by Gavarni and his predecessors were not designs by the artists but representations of realised ideas created by often anonymous dressmakers. With few exceptions, such as Rose Bertin and Leroy, who made clothes for Queen Marie-Antoinette and the Empress Josephine respectively, the dressmaker was regarded in the main simply as a tradesman—the era of the 'grand couturier' was still to come with the rise of Charles Frederick Worth.

The Industrial Revolution and the rise of a newly prosperous middle class had the simultaneous effect of creating an abundance of machine-made objects and a ready market for them among an emergent public, eager to show off their prosperity by a display of possessions which were only too often ill-designed and overburdened with inappropriate ornament. Just as the interior decorations of the middle decades of the nineteenth century became more and more encumbered with a mass of unnecessary and over-elaborate furniture and bric-à-brac, so the tendency of women's clothes was to become equally ostentatious in their demonstration of family wealth. This trend was to be seen at its best or worst among the mainly new rich and often dubious society centering round the court of Napoleon the Third. The simple dresses of the opening years of the century gave way to vast swaying crinolines decorated with a plethora of frills, swags, braids and tassels. Innumerable sewing women were needed to finish by hand even the simplest crinoline.

The sewing machine in a primitive form had been invented in 1830 by Barthelmy Thimonnier but was not practical for general purposes as it was only capable of sewing a chain stitch which had the disadvantage of coming undone if the single thread used were inadvertently pulled.

28 Valentine Gross Models by Chéruit, Martial et Armand, Worth and Jenny. *Gazette du Bon Ton,* 1915.

A Boston mechanic, Elias Howe, improved on Thimonnier's concept and in 1846 he patented a machine which, while still cumbrous, worked with a double thread to make a lockstitch which would not unravel as easily as chain stitch. Howe failed to interest manufacturers in either America or England but Elias Singer, also from Boston, improved Howe's model making it more adaptable and easier to work. Patented in 1851 the Singer machine was mass-produced and sold to housewives as well as to clothing manufacturers. But the average housewife armed with fabric and her new sewing machine still needed models which could be copied, simplified or improvised upon. Thus the demand for illustrated fashion magazines increased and during the eighteen-fifties housewives and professional dressmakers could purchase such periodicals as *Les Modes Parisiennes, Le Moniteur de la Mode* or *Le Follet* which brought the latest Paris fashions to the most remote hamlet, to be interpreted according to the skill available. Reproduced as engravings or lithographs, often coloured by hand, the original drawings by Héloïse Leloir, Jules David and Anaïs Toudouze—to mention the most adept of the many fashion illustrators of the time—have great charm and freshness.

It is a curious fact that when fashion changes drastically the tendency is for fashion journals to disappear with the old style and to be replaced by newcomers. A good example of this can be seen in the *Gazette du Bon Ton* which recorded the decorative fashions from 1912 onward but went out of publication in 1925 with the advent of the short skirt and a general trend to simplicity. Earlier the change from the crinoline to the bustle gave rise to such new publications as *Le Miroir Parisien* and *Le Petit Courier des Dames* (the invention of new names for each fresh journal must have given rise to the exercise of considerable ingenuity). One of the longest running magazines, *Le Mode Artistique*, appeared in 1877 and survived into the twentieth

VI Etienne Drian 'La Marseillaise.' Elegant patriotism stressed by the choice of colouring in a drawing for the *Gazette du Bon Ton,* 1915. Drian was much in demand in the 'twenties and 'thirties for his sanguine portrait drawings and decorative murals.

century. *Nouveautés Parisiennes, La Nouvelle Mode, Salon de la Mode* and *La Mode Illustrée* recorded the fashions of the 'nineties as did *Fémina* for the early years of the twentieth century. The standard of draughtsmanship had sadly deteriorated, however, and the clothes are on models mechanically drawn with insipid expressions, simpering with tiny mouths and enormous eyes, the waists excessively small and the anatomy in general non-existent. Little individuality can be detected and fashion illustration was at its lowest ebb. The reason for this can be seen in the increasing use of photographs by Reutlinger, Félix and Talbot. Even drawings bearing the signatures of de Billy, Jane Durelle, Félix Desgranges, René, Fabiano or Mlle. Bert, are rarely above a common level of mediocrity. However, in 1908 there appeared *Les Robes de Paul Poiret,* a slim volume illustrated by a young artist named Paul Iribe, which set a new standard.

opposite
VII Georges Lepape 'Le Miroir Rouge'. Colour plate issued *hors-texte* in *Feuillets d'Art,* 1919. Lepape has conventionalised the face of his model to resemble a traditional Japanese Noh mask. The drawing is bordered by an orange line as in his drawings for *Les Choses de Paul Poiret,* executed eight years before.

30 Charles Martin Advertisement for Tecla jewellery, 1913.

Primarily Paul Poiret's object was to publicise his couture house and draw attention to his revolutionary ideas by producing an elegantly discreet booklet. This was in itself an innovation—one of the many which would spring from his fertile imagination. There could well have been another aim, that of rivalling the artistic reputation of his idol and one-time employer, Jacques Doucet, from whom he had learnt so much.

Jean-François Revel in an article on Doucet's career as a couturier and connoisseur of the arts points out that during the Second Empire the dressmaker emerged from the ranks of tradesmen to take his place among 'the *monstres sacrés* of our society'. Charles Frederick Worth was the first to make this decisive step over the lines dividing society. A circumstance in Worth's favour, apart from his talent as a designer, was that society was less rigid at the court of Napoleon the Third than at almost any other time in French history. With the patronage of the Empress Eugénie and celebrities of great beauty but small reputation he was able to join the rather louche circle around the Emperor and Empress—a position he maintained even after the disasters of the Franco-Prussian war and the enforced exile of many of his erstwhile patrons.

Edmond de Goncourt records that in 1872 he was astonished by the number of carriages outside a house in the rue de la Paix—'as many as at a première at the Théâtre-Français'—and discovered that they were waiting for Worth's clients. De Goncourt was even more surprised to find that a cousin, living a very secluded life in the country, had dresses made by Worth not to wear but to hang in her wardrobes to show visiting neighbours. In 1882 he was taken by Princess Mathilde to visit Worth in 'his ridiculous fairy palace' where 'the walls were completely covered with china plates of every period and country' (25,000 according to Madame Worth), and where the chairs were covered with crystal bead fringes, and cut glass salad bowls replaced the windowpanes. This 'delirium of broken china and carafe stoppers' Worth was unable to enjoy to the full on returning home from his salon, for according to Madame Worth he was incapable even of eating owing to the severe migraines brought on by the odours, natural and artificial, of his clients.

At the time of the de Goncourt visit to Worth's house the latter was 63. Worth's background had been a small dreary town in Lincolnshire, and his childhood one of miserable poverty owing to the gambling debts of a thriftless father. He had been forced to leave school at the age of eleven to work in a printer's. All this was in strict contrast to the life of his successor

31,32 Etienne Drian *Hors-texte* plates in *Gazette du Bon Ton*. They do not appear to represent actual models but were possibly included for their style and elegance.

as a leader of fashion, Jacques Doucet, who was already making his mark in his twenties. On arriving in London, still no more than a child, Worth made his first acquaintance with the world of luxury in the firm of Lewis and Allenby, while Doucet continued to enjoy the comfortable prosperity derived from the family business of fine laces which had been started in 1824 by his grandfather in the rue de la Paix. Over the years the family business had attracted an extremely distinguished following, numbering among its clients the crowned heads and aristocracy of England, France and Russia.

Worth's taste in interior decoration may have amused de Goncourt and his circle, all of whom were rediscovering the neglected masterpieces of the eighteenth century and were enthralled by examples of Japanese art recently introduced into Europe but the fact was that Worth's formative years were spent among a society devoted to excess and display. Taste had drastically altered —and the writings of the de Goncourts had played a significant part in this—by the time Doucet had time to spare from consolidating the success of his couture business to concentrate on his personal interest in the arts. Once launched on a course as a collector Doucet became the possessor of paintings and drawings by Boucher, Fragonard and Watteau, sculpture by Houdon and Clodion and furniture by Jacob, Weisweiller and the finest cabinet-makers of the previous century. His reputation as a connoisseur grew but although he kept his two interests apart he found that the fact that he was a dressmaker effectively prevented his being invited to a number of aristocratic houses. The story went that perhaps rather unwisely he enquired why he had never been invited to the home of a fellow collector and received the chilling reply that it would not be proper for him to meet socially women he had seen in their underwear in his fitting rooms.

Doucet suddenly sold his collection in 1912. It was rumoured that his house, furnished to the last detail with the finest artifacts and paintings of the eighteenth century, had been intended as a setting for a lady with whom he had been deeply in love for many years but circumstances prevented him from marrying. After years of waiting she became free to become Madame Doucet but very soon after was tragically killed in a hunting accident. But perhaps this story was a romantic fiction and the probable truth is that Doucet, like many collectors, had reached the limits of that particular interest and needed new outlets. This time he turned his attention to the work of more recent times. *La Charmeuse des Serpents* by Douanier Rousseau, *Les Demoiselles*

34 **Georges Lepape** Portrait of a young man, 1918. Reproduced in *Feuillets d'Art,* 1919.

35 Benito Dinner dress in satin, the skirt cut to form 'jupes-culottes' (cf. ills. 7 and 46). Wide jade green ribbons form hip draperies and fall in panels. Designer not named. Drawn in 1919 for the first issue of *Gazette du Bon Ton,* February 1920. The magazine appeared regularly after the War.

d'Avignon by Picasso, and Seurat's *Le Cirque* were among the most notable of his new acquisitions, made with the advice of André Breton. Canvases by Max Ernst and Chirico were set off by furniture, rugs and bookbindings specially designed and executed by the foremost craftsmen of the day. Many of these found a permanent home in the Musée des Arts Décoratifs after Doucet's death in 1929, which passed almost unnoticed in the French press despite his munificent gifts of thousands of rare books on eighteenth century costume which he had given to the University of Paris. Jacques Doucet's passion for collecting, his patronage of the decorative arts and his personal elegance were decisive influences on the young Paul Poiret. In the latter's autobiography Doucet is always referred to with sincere respect and admiration. Doucet was his master '. . . it was a great honour to have been his pupil', while his appreciation and praise stimulated Poiret to work harder than ever. Doucet, 'the perfection of handsomeness and elegance, exceedingly soigné and looking as though he had just come out of a bandbox', was, for the nineteen-year old Poiret, 'the man I wished to become . . . I did not want any other model in life but him . . . I would have liked to make myself in his image'.

As a result of his work for Doucet Poiret came into contact with the notabilities of the day, particularly the actresses and *grandes-cocottes* (more often than not the two careers were simultaneous) and their rich protectors. He not only learned the art of dressing the most beautiful and striking women in Paris but also, under Doucet's guidance, how to dress himself. Naturally Doucet's enthusiasm for the arts infected him though with the difference that whereas Doucet had kept his life as a couturier and that as a collector in separate compartments Poiret combined the two.

Poiret's desire to emulate his master inevitably became an even stronger desire to surpass him and the heady delights of publicity gave birth to the idea of 'bringing out a very beautifully produced publication intended for the élite of Society . . . dedicated in homage to all the great ladies of the world'. The choice of artist to illustrate his creations fell upon the young Paul

36 Benito Decorative *cul-de-lampe. Feuillets d'Art,* 1919.

Dessin de Mario Simon pour le dernier parfum de Rosine

ANTINÉA
OU
AU
FOND
DE
LA
MER

ROSINE
PARIS

Iribe whose work for the short-lived periodical *Le Témoin* had attracted favourable notice. Iribe was twenty-five.

Les Robes de Paul Poiret was completed in October 1908, in an edition of two hundred and fifty copies, priced at 40 francs. It consisted of ten full-page drawings by Iribe, reproduced in colour, had no text and was bound in cream-coloured boards. The cover bore only a narrow, rather conventional design in black of an oval plaque with thin garlands of roses—the same roses formed by an irregular spiral line which became one of the most characteristic motifs of Art Deco—the plaque enclosing the legend *les Robes de Paul Poiret racontées par Paul Iribe* in vermilion—a design repeated on the title page. Iribe used a similar version of this cartouche for an advertisement for the scent *Quelle Fleur* two years later, while the garlands of flowers re-appear in a drawing for another scent *Ilka*, launched by Piver in 1911.

The *justification de tirage* was accompanied by two tiny sketches in terracotta of an empty, striped dressmaker's box with the interlaced initials 'P.P.' and the silhouette of a pelican with the initials of Iribe and the date, 1908. The plates, all of which were coloured by the *pochoir* process, show the background and furniture in black line, the colour being restricted to the figures. A narrow range of colours, deep in tone but slightly muted, was used with freedom and in some cases the hair of the models is either terracotta or an improbable shade of purple.

Without exception the plates reflect Poiret's revolutionary ideas concerning fashion and follow a general line of long, straight, high-waisted dresses with tight sleeves. Ornament is reduced to a minimum and the derivation from the Directoire and Empire fashions, with their neo-classical and English influences, is very marked. The coiffures resemble the short hair styles of the Revolutionary period and feature an encircling band of fabric in a colour contrasting with the dress. Not only were the dresses at the greatest variance with current fashions, but their apparent simplicity of cut and fabric were far removed from the elaborate ruffled and ornamented toilettes of Poiret's rivals. The figures themselves are shown without the corsets worn—or rather endured—by fashionable women. Even the models are radically different in features. Iribe's young women have half-closed eyes and smile with an almost sly expression as though amused at their own thoughts. Attention has been paid to the furniture and objects which contribute so much to the novel atmosphere of the drawings. A convex mirror reflects a somewhat sinister orchid in an exotic vase; a Vermeer painting and a Régence caned chair almost dominate

Kalyf

parfum

exquis

BRUNELLESCHI.

another drawing; what could be a framed design by Fernand Khnopf and a Chinese incense burner in the shape of a toad, engage the attention of the models in another plate while a Romney portrait of Emma Hamilton, an Italian Directoire commode and a bronze nude serve as décor for a classically simple white evening-dress, dramatised by a pink rose and matching headband. The oriental influence which was to become such a dominant feature of Poiret's designs is anticipated in a sketch of a turban with an aigrette and a design for three evening cloaks.

Poiret tells in his autobiography of the difficulties he had experienced with Paul Iribe during the preparation of the book. There were constant delays due to the latter's slowness in producing the drawings and to the artist's lack of a fixed address; letters only reached Iribe through a mysterious Madame L. with whom he breakfasted every morning. Iribe must in fact have had a working studio, but deliberately kept its address unknown to Poiret to protect himself from interference; by producing the designs only at the last moment he made sure that no last-minute alterations could be dictated!

In spite of its small circulation the volume had a considerable impact and its sympathetic realisation of Poiret's concepts gave rise to rumours which caused the couturier no small annoyance, as he duly records in his autobiography. 'A venemous Parisian newspaper' insinuated that Poiret's 'personal genius' was in reality the work of Paul Iribe and, rather inexplicably, Marie Laurencin. Poiret's attempts to obtain a denial from Iribe of this calumny were foiled by his continued ignorance of the latter's whereabouts—an odd fact when Iribe was working for a number of periodicals and advertisers who appeared to have been able to reach him without any difficulty. He seems to have found a more serene and fruitful occupation in his elegant furniture designs, done for Jacques Doucet's studio in the avenue de Bois. After his departure

Croquis N° V

Gazette du Bon ton N° 1 · JANV. 1920.

41 Guy Arnoux Illustration to an article by René Kerdyk, *Fémina-Noël,* 1920.

42 Alexandre Rzewuski Illustration to an article by Pierre de Trévières, *Fémina-Noël,* 1920.

VIII Marthe Romme Colour plate from *Feuillets d'Art,* 1919. Gouache drawing by an artist who worked for *Feuillets d'Art* and *Gazette du Bon Ton* in the early 'twenties. The oriental inspiration of Léon Bakst's designs for the Ballets Russes was still dominant in the postwar period and the accent on the hips by draped panniers was characteristic of the early 'twenties.

43 André Marty Illustration to an article by Dominique Sylvaire, *Fémina-Noël,* 1920.

in 1914 for the United States Iribe worked for the theatre and the movies until 1930 when he returned to France, and, among other work, designed jewellery for Chanel (according to Jean Cocteau, he had started work as an assistant to René Lalique, the great Art Nouveau jeweller). Three years later Poiret embarked upon another book but in the meantime the artistic scene in Paris had been pervaded with a new influence.

opposite
IX George Barbier 'Laissez-moi-seule! Colour plate from *Feuillets d'Art,* 1919. Barbier was an ardent admirer of the Ballets Russes and did many portrait drawings of its leading dancers in their various roles. This decorative drawing, though not a representation of an actual couture model, sums up the current trends in fashion and textile design.

Les Bijoux Excentriques

45 Benito Illustration to an article by Paul Géraldy, *Fémina-Noël,* 1920.

46 Pierre Brissaud 'Viendra-t-il?', *Gazette du Bon Ton,* 1920. Evening dress of white crêpe designed by Beer with panniers of black and silver striped fabric. The extremely low cut back is typical of the 'naked' fashions of the immediately postwar years and in this model Beer attempted a revival of the 'jupes-culottes', fashionable between 1910 and 1911.

opposite
44   Benito Illustration to an article by Gerard Bauer, *Fémina-Noël,* 1920.

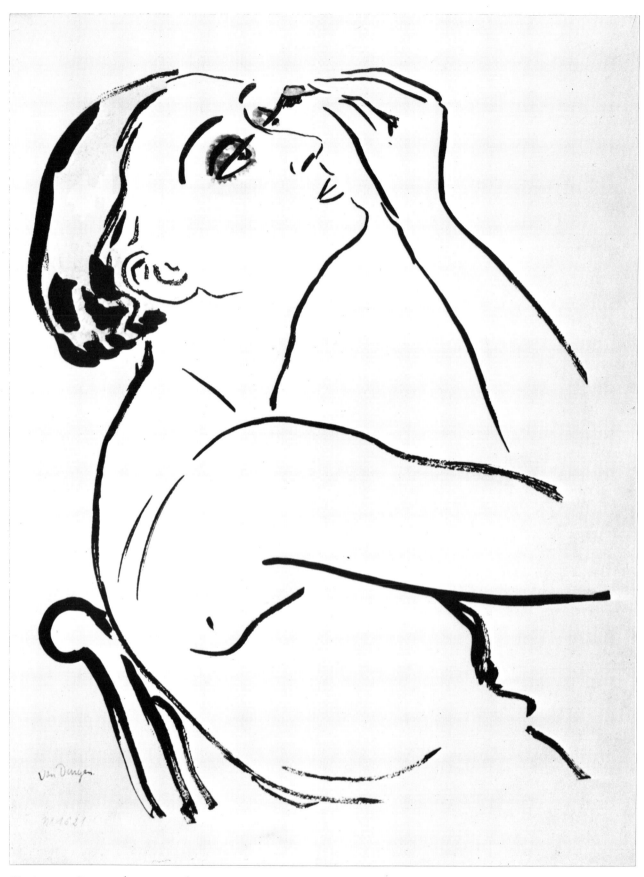

47 **Kees van Dongen** 'Le Rimmel', *Feuillets d'Art,* 1920. *Hors-texte* lithograph.

3

FROM the seventeenth century Parisian taste with its insatiable appetite for the exotic and the fantastic had drawn on oriental themes from which motifs were incorporated into contemporary decorative arts. From China, legendary and mysterious, from Japan, forbidden to Europeans except for one precariously held Dutch trading post, came porcelains and lacquer to be placed in precious bronze-doré mounts and amalgamated into furniture. Artifacts of the more accessible regions of the Near East had been indiscriminately labelled Turkish and Persian, while their decorative arts were similarly used to inspire plays, ballets, operas, novels and interior decorations. Intrepid painters faced hardships to record scenes of life in Arabia and Persia and in the nineteenth century serried ranks of paintings with oriental themes crowded the walls of the annual Salons in Paris. The contemporary taste for objects overburdened with ornament gave ample scope for versions of oriental motifs, the originals being as eagerly collected as the pastiches.

Thus the oriental themes, introduced by the Ballets Russes when they arrived in Paris in 1909, were not an especially new and dazzling revelation for a Parisian public already familiar with the stories of *The Arabian Nights* from the translations of Dr. Mardrus. Indeed there were already a number of productions to be seen in the theatre which had explored the same vein such as *Sumurun* produced by Max Reinhardt, *Kismet* and *Les Trois Sultanes*. It was more the treatment of these themes in such ballets as *Thamar* and in particular *Schéhérazade* which made such an overwhelming impression. The daring combinations of brilliant sensuous colours which were an inherent element in Léon Bakst's designs for costumes and décor, the unfamiliar and exciting music of Rimsky-Korsakov and Balakirev, the passionate abandon of Michel Fokine's choreography combined with the personal beauty and dazzling techniques of Nijinsky and Ida Rubinstein produced an effect on the first night audience which no ballet before or since could equal. Jacques-Emile Blanche, the painter, critic and one of the sponsors of the Ballets Russes, wrote some twenty years later that 'the first performance of *Schéhérazade* was an important evening for the theatre, for dressmakers, for interior decorators, for jewellers and for all branches of decoration. It is difficult today to realise the metamorphosis which transformed the decorative arts'. Even more ecstatic praise was lavished by critics and writers in 1910. Paris was ripe for a new inspiration. The quick demise of Art Nouveau very soon after the 1900 Exhibition had left a decorative vacuum characterised by a timid return to eight-

48 Benito Evening dress of russet satin and gold lace, *Gazette du Bon Ton,* 1920. Couturier unnamed. A cosmetic detail is the rouging of the tips of the fingers fashionable in the early 'twenties.

opposite
49 André Marty 'La Soubrette Annamite', *Gazette du Bon Ton,* 1920. Doeuillet evening dress embroidered with sequins in a geometrical design, the ribbon drapery having Persian motifs woven in pale blue and pink.

eenth century themes and a period of insipid banality in both fashion and decoration. In 1910, the same year as the première of *Schéhérazade,* there had been the influential exhibition of modern decorative art from Munich which, despite critical disdain occasioned by anti-German feelings, had proved immensely popular. From this exhibition and from the Ballets Russes came the two main characteristics of Art Deco.

The oriental influence was more immediately apparent in fashion, a trend encouraged by Paul Poiret who claimed that he alone was responsible for the craze for brilliant, richly-textured fabrics, the *jupes-culottes* or trouser skirts, reminiscent of those worn by the inhabitants of Shah Shariah's harem, the endless ropes of pearls, and the turbans decked with costly aigrettes which Parisiennes adopted so eagerly. Whether Bakst or Poiret was the originator, the effect was immediate. The subdued and even drab hues of grey, navy blue, prune, kaki (*sic*), olive and myrtle green mentioned in descriptions of dresses early in 1910 were very soon replaced by more exciting shades of begonia rose, cerise, jonquil, Delft blue, rose vif and Nuit d'Orient—a rich deep ultramarine. The vivid green of jade or emeralds and a particularly hard shade of orange—in a slightly muted tone to be called 'tango' in the 'twenties—were two innovations seen everywhere.

The taste for the exotic extended as a matter of course to scents. The new dresses needed a more pungent accompaniment than the discreet and bland flower perfumes which had hitherto been considered suitable for respectable ladies. Now that chic women were anxious to look like odalisques something more heady was needed to suit the prevailing passion for the world of *The Arabian Nights.* Once again Paul Poiret was quick to sense the demand and the heavy cloying perfumes, fashionable long ago during the Second Empire, and which had caused Worth so much suffering, were redistilled again. Based on sandalwood, patchouli and cloves the new scents were combined with chemical essences to create more subtle essences. They were given appropriately sultry names: Poiret's 'L'Etrange Fleur', 'Maharadjah' and 'Antinéa ou Au

50 Edouard Halouze Drawing showing the trends in men's fashions. Although dated by the artist '1920' it was actually published as a supplement in a 1919 issue of *Feuillets d'Art.*

51 Georges Lepape Advertisement for the scent 'Fleur de France', sold by Orsay, 1920.

52, 53 Lerus? A draped white satin evening dress with coral lace back drapery and a short train; an evening dress in 'vieux-rouge' lamé and black satin with an overblouse made of a network of jet beads. *L'Illustration des Modes,* 1920. Name of the couturier not mentioned.

Fond de la Mer', Guerlain's 'Mitsuoko', Legrand's 'Balkis' and 'l'Yperlée', Fouillat's 'Son Péché'—described as a 'parfum diabolique', Babani's 'La Rose Gullistan' and 'L'Ambre de Delhi' were some of these new scents while Bichara's 'Sakountala' and 'Nirvana' were guaranteed to 'give the voluptuous feelings of the Ballets Russes and to conjure in our memories the choreographic and decorative seductions of *Schéhérazade*'! To publicise these scents such talents as those of Paul Iribe, Georges Lepape, Mario Simon and Umberto Brunelleschi were enlisted before and immediately after the war and their help was sought in designing the elaborate containers for the scent bottles made by Lalique and Baccarat.

It was in this new artistic climate that three years later Paul Poiret embarked on another booklet, this time more ambitious in design. This time he engaged the twenty-four year old Georges Lepape, who had studied at the Beaux-Arts in the Atelier Corman. Lepape, André Marty, Pierre Brissaud and Charles Martin were fellow students. It is curious that they should have spent a large part of their careers depicting elegant women in the latest fashions after having been under the tuition of Fernand-Piestre Corman who achieved considerable fame with his vast canvases peopled with prehistoric men and women clothed in ragged goatskins, their hair

54 Illegible signature Advertisement for J. Seurre, Paris, 1921

matted and unkempt. Despite these gloomy and long forgotten works, Corman was an amiable and amusing teacher who gained the affection of his pupils among whom were Toulouse-Lautrec, van Gogh, Sérusier, Matisse and Picabia.

Poiret was reticent in his autobiography about the creation of *Les Choses de Paul Poiret* as the work was called on its appearance in 1911, devoting only a single paragraph to the subject but in this he emphasises the influence he had had over the artist and stresses 'the marvellous opportunity he had given Lepape'. Certainly Lepape proved one of the most prolific and sought after fashion illustrators, both in the years immediately prior to the First World War and during the 'twenties and 'thirties when he contributed to *Vogue, Harper's Bazaar, Fémina, L'Illustration,* and *Vanity Fair*. He also illustrated *éditions de luxe* and designed sets and costumes for revues, plays and films. In this, his most important commission for Poiret, he already displays a developed and consistent style and a command of colour both original and audacious. *Les Choses de Paul Poiret* undoubtedly opened up new vistas in drawing the attention of a dis-

criminating section of the public to his work, but like Iribe he was under the spell of the Ballets Russes. This could not have endeared him to Poiret who considered Bakst in his oriental themes something of a pasticheur of his own work. However, Lepape lasted longer in Poiret's esteem than Iribe and in 1920 designed a striking poster for the 'Tour d'Europe' when Poiret and his models embarked on a publicity trip.

Les Choses de Paul Poiret, larger in format than its predecessor, was published in a bigger edition of one thousand copies printed on *papier de luxe* of which the first three hundred were numbered and initialled by Poiret and in addition had three plates printed on paper from the Imperial Manufactory of Japan. These were for sale at a price of fifty francs. The striking cover on cream paper bears a drawing in black of an intricate arrangement of knots and tassels, not, as has been stated, designed by Poiret himself but actually of a traditional Japanese pattern. This forms a vertical motif which is balanced by the title in vermilion and here it is noticeable that Lepape's name is in the same size type as that of Poiret whereas in the previous volume Iribe's name had been in letters so small as to be barely legible. Again on the first page couturier and artist are represented by a small drawing, Poiret by a black and white lamp with an orange key-patterned shade and Lepape by a short umbrella. The plates themselves are extremely colourful—black being entirely absent. In some cases gold and silver metallic ink was used.

Poiret is still continuing and developing the theme of long tight dresses with a high waist line but the bouffant coiffures of 1908 have been replaced by turbans which completely cover the hair except for a few straggling locks 'à la façon de Madame Tallien'. A certain influence of Japanese prints can be seen in the drawing of the models, as supple and boneless as cats with half-closed eyes and tiny mouths. The asymmetrical arrangement of the figures is again reminiscent of Japanese prints and in one plate a model appears to be walking out of the picture. A version of Poiret's salon appears as a background, its white walls with pilasters and door-frames picked out in a deep turquoise green, providing a foil for a girl in a terracotta dress with

56 Alexandre Rzewuski   Wedding dress of silver tissue over white lace caught at the waist line with a pearl buckle; the white lace veil decorated with sprays of orange blossom.   Designed by Worth and included in a 'Marriage' number of *Gazette du Bon Ton,* 1921.

57 Etienne Drian   Paul Poiret designs for a bride of the future and her bridesmaid.   From the 'Marriage' number of *Gazette du Bon Ton,* 1921.   These designs were realised for and worn by the Dolly Sisters in a 'Brides of the Future' number of *The League of Notions* revue devised by Charles B. Cochran, for whom Poiret often designed special costumes. In spite of the title these models are reminiscent of the travesty costumes of the period of Louis XIV, an epoch much to the taste of Drian himself.

58 **Pierre Mourgue** Illustration to an article by Marcel Astruc on the use of straw as a decorative accessory.

a cyclamen-mauve turban. In another drawing a blonde model in a white dress reclines sensuously on a pile of cushions in shades of rose pink, blue and green. Apart from the turbans—and a striking example of one of these can be seen in the beautiful head of a girl wearing a silver spotted and beaded headdress with a white aigrette—the oriental influence is marked. A girl in a stylish canary-yellow dress banded with fur at the cuffs and hem and girdled with an orange cord holds an emerald green parrot while accepting the offering of a Negro page clad in a harmony of soft blues, green and pink; three models—one clad in a tunic dress patterned with Art Deco roses—are shown in the blue and green striped box of a theatre where a performance of a ballet, possibly *Cléopâtre,* is taking place while in a folding plate showing various accessories there are references in the captions to 'the Chinese taste'. A version of a Chinese coolie hat forms part of the trousered ensembles featured in 'Celles de Demain'. Here Poiret forecasts the wearing of trousers more resembling those worn by men than the current *jupes-culottes* which were like divided skirts. For gardening he suggested trousers in butcher blue

59 **J. Simont** 'Parisiennes en promenade au Parc de Saint-Cloud', *L'Illustration,* 1921.

striped fabric with a yellow waistcoat and the Chinese coolie hat in a shade of orange; for tennis in white with a green scarf and belt; for walking orange trousers with wide bands of the fur which trims a short orange buttoned jacket over a white high collared blouse and finally for evening a parma violet sleeveless tunic over a pair of emerald green trousers. The unconventional combinations of brilliant colours and particularly the Persian inspired use of blue and green could well have inspired Marcel Proust to put into the mouth of M. de Charlus the words 'Only women who do not know how to dress are afraid of colours'.

These two volumes published by Poiret had considerable influence despite their slim contents and comparatively small editions. The lack of any printed text concentrated the attention on the illustrations and the name of Poiret, the creator of avant-garde fashions, would have alone guaranteed their being taken seriously by the world of fashion. There can be little doubt that they were the inspiration for more commercial fashion magazines which made their appearance in 1912, *Gazette du Bon Ton, Le Journal des Dames et des Modes* and *Modes et Manières d'Aujourd'hui,* all with titles reminiscent of their predecessors in the eighteenth and nineteenth centuries.

Edna Woolman Chase, a former editor of *Vogue,* tells of the founding of the *Gazette du Bon Ton* in her memoirs *Always in Vogue.* Lucien Vogel, a publisher much involved in the world of Paris couture, happened to be staying in the country house of Madame Vogel's cousin. They were installed in the bedroom usually occupied by an absent friend of their host. This friend was related to three young painters and was a great admirer of their work which covered the walls of the room. Vogel was struck by the quality of the different paintings and drawings and remarked on the sympathetic feeling for fashion which pervaded them all. The idea occurred to him that these young artists should devote their talents to illustrating fashion in a new

X Pierre Brissaud 'La Fête est Finie.' Colour plate from *Gazette du Bon Ton,* 1920. Organdie dresses for mother and child, designed by Jeanne Lanvin, who started her career as a dressmaker by designing clothes for her small daughter. These were admired by the clients visiting her hatshop in the faubourg Saint-Honoré, which she opened in 1890. Jeanne Lanvin later extended her talents to interior decoration and part of the furnishings and decor of her house in Paris, which was designed as a setting for her collection of contemporary paintings, is now in the Musée des Arts Décoratifs.

XI *Above left:* **Mario Simon** 'La Pluie d'Or.' Colour plate from *Feuillets d'Art,* 1920. Couturier unnamed but possibly Poiret for whom Simon drew the advertisement (see ill. 37) for perfume. Simon also worked for Poiret's Atelier Martine.

XII *Above:* **Jean Dupas** Catalogue cover for an American department store, 1928

XIII *Left:* **Charles Martin** Drawing illustrating a proverb commissioned by *Fémina* for the Christmas 1920 number. Martin was 72 when this drawing was executed and until his death in 1934 worked continuously on fashion drawings, murals and book illustrations with a sure and original touch.

60 **P.W.** Hat designed by Camille Roger. *Gazette du Bon Ton,* 1921.

periodical which he would publish. To the original three, Bernard Boutet de Monval, Jacques and Pierre Brissaud, were added George Barbier, André Marty, Charles Martin, Georges Lepape and for a short time Paul Iribe. These formed the nucleus of illustrators and additional drawings came from Carlègle, Paul Méras, Gosé, Soulié, Guy Arnoux, Robert Dammy,

61 Pierre Brissaud 'Conte des Fées'. Evening dress and child's dress designed by Jeanne Lanvin, who had entered the world of couture as a result of the admiration given to the dresses she made for her own daughter. Afterwards she extended her range to dresses for adults.

Strimpl, Etienne Drian and Erté.

Conceived in terms of the finest hand-made paper, the most elegant typography and the finest reproduction of drawings which were often hand-coloured, the *Gazette du Bon Ton* also contained short articles by Gabriel Moury, Jean-Louis Vaudoyer, Roger Boutet de Monval, Claude Roger Marx, René Blum and Jean Giraudoux among others, in which various aspects of fashion were examined in a somewhat cursory manner and illustrated with thumbnail sketches. Little or no practical information was given and the impression is left that these poeti-

62 Anonymous Paper fan, 1921. Printed paper fans, often commissioned from the leading designers and made by the distinguished firm of Duvellroy, were given away as souvenirs of special occasions by hotels and restaurants in London, Paris and Monte-Carlo. They were also used as advertisements (and in this case were made of scented paper) by the better known parfumiers.

63 Robert Polack Paper fan, 1921.

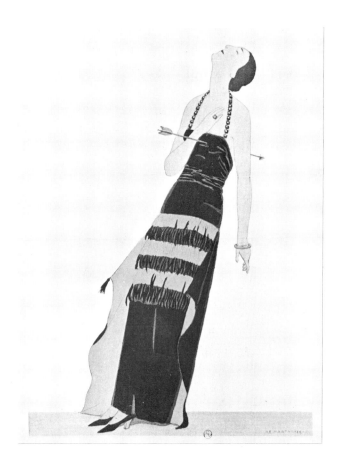

cal and imaginative effusions were included more for the prestige value of the authors's names than for any penetrating information about the philosophy of fashion. The full-page coloured plates, on an average ten to a number, were of course the main attraction of the magazine,

Chase states, 'a casualty of the First World War' and neither, as is often stated, was it completely discontinued during the hostilities.

War or no war, Paris was determined that her role of arbiter and absolute dictator of fashion should not be allowed to be usurped. The necessary materials might be difficult to obtain, many of the *maisons de couture* might be temporarily closed and skilled labour growing scarcer but it was as much a matter of national pride as it was a question of national economy, that since the seventeenth century Paris had pulled the strings to which elegant women danced. The international Exhibition held in San Francisco in 1915, far from the tensions of Europe, offered an opportunity for the Parisian houses of Beer, Callot, Martial et Armand, Doucet, Jenny, Worth, Chéruit, Paquin and Premet to demonstrate French pre-eminence in design and, incidently, to explore new markets. The occasion was recorded in a special number of the *Gazette du Bon Ton* and this particular issue dated 15 June 1915—'the 316th day of the war'—showed no lowering of the standards of pre-war numbers and was infused with a euphoric and, in view of later events, misplaced optimism. 'Although part of French soil is still occupied by the invaders Paris is still the Paris of Good Taste and Fashion', declared an editorial, continuing that 'France has escaped the greatest peril and marches toward certain victory allowing feminine coquetry to reveal a delicious smile'. Still further numbers intending to show the fashions Paris considered appropriate to the troubled times were planned and the editors obviously considered that the war would be over before the end of the year (significantly, the subscription rates were still indicated on the final page). Many of the usual artists contributed drawings

65 Georges Lepape 'Le Bon Accueil', *Gazette du Bon Ton,* 1922. Afternoon dress in black moiré with white organdie frills. Designed by Martial et Armand.

which were reproduced with customary expertise—Charles Martin, Georges Lepape, Etienne Drian, George Barbier as well as a newcomer, Valentine Gross, who had had her first exhibition at the Galerie Théâtre des Champs-Elysées in 1913. Like most of her contemporaries an ardent dévotée of the Ballets Russes, Valentine Gross had recorded a number of ballets but her black and white line drawings of the models sent to San Francisco were not as distinguished for their elegance as those of the other contributors and she seems to have accentuated the worst qualities of the modes of 1915 which were, admittedly, not particularly attractive and even clumsy. A typical silhouette combined an extremely full skirt of mid-calf length, the fullness starting from a high waistline and a waistcoat bodice with an accentuated collar which gave a vaguely military effect. These full skirts were, it was claimed, to allow for free movement in walking as cars were no longer available owing to wartime conditions. 'The car having disappeared from everyday life since the war, the walking costume has predictably become fashionable and has taken on shapes inspired by the simple practical clothes of cowboys, page-boys or jockeys'. The 'insolent' aigrettes which took Paris by storm as a result of the Ballets Russes disappeared to be replaced by versions of the tricorne or more military forms. Boots with moderately high heels provided protection and comfort to those forced to indulge in the unaccustomed effort of walking. Muslin, organdie and tulle were much in use for day wear —rather perversely in view of the existing conditions—and these were embroidered and re-embroidered 'as we have never seen before' while for evening dresses the richest of metal embroidered fabrics were combined with silver or gold lace. The *Gazette du Bon Ton* stated that such elaborate toilettes were eminently suitable for attending concerts in hospitals for 'we must make ourselves as beautiful as we can for the wounded . . . we must strike a contrast with the grim, depressing surrounding of the hospital wards'.

66 George Barbier 'Sortilèges', *Gazette du Bon Ton,* 1922. Evening dress designed by Beer in beaded blue lamé over silver tissue. Barbier specialised in elaborate backgrounds (cf. plate IX), which, to avoid overwhelming the central figure he treated in a contrasting range of colours, in this case subdued tones of orange and russet.

WHEN hostilities ceased, the stock-taking began and the map of Europe had to be redrawn. Four kings had been deposed, two empires had collapsed into ruin, three new republics had come into existence and apart from those countries fortunate enough to maintain their neutrality, the protagonists had emerged burdened with almost insuperable economic problems which were exacerbated by bitter resentments. France had suffered devastation at the hands of the invading forces in the formerly prosperous manufacturing areas of the north and those factories which had not been totally destroyed had been looted: valuable equipment and machinery had been sent to Germany to be converted into armaments. Gigantic claims for compensation and reparations had been made against a totally bankrupt and defeated enemy but the immediate problem was to resume production to prevent France herself, exhausted by the war, from sinking into the condition of her late and ever-to-be hated enemy. For a spell the menace of trade competition with Germany was removed and Paris, though hampered by shortages of labour and materials, at least had the satisfaction of knowing that no other European capital could oust her from her traditional position as a leader of fashion. As a matter of necessity the fashion industry, so vital to the economy of the country, was set in motion as a priority. The woollen manufacturers in the north of France had been among the gravest casualties but the silk weaving industry centred around Lyons, both in large factories and innumerable small homes, was only marginally affected by a shortage of skilled labour. Paris shook off the drab atmosphere which so depressed the English couturière Lucile when she returned there immediately after the war to reopen her Parisian branch, and gradually the intricate mechanism of the fashion world began once again to resume its pre-war pace and to recapture its former mystique.

It is a popular misconception that the moment peace was declared women drastically shortened their skirts to symbolise the new freedoms which they had won during the war. In fact seven years elapsed before the knee-length skirts which have come to characterise the decade were introduced in the winter of 1925 and before that the hemlines had dropped from mid-calf in 1919 to ankle length in 1923. Four interminable years of war had not dulled the taste for luxury which had marked the pre-war era; memories of the quasi-oriental fantasies inspired by the Ballets Russes were renewed when Diaghilev's company once more introduced the lure of *Schéhérazade* to new audiences. Fashion designers continued, at least for a year or more,

67 **Pierre Mourgue** 'Deux Coups de Chapeau', *Gazette du Bon Ton,* 1922. Men's tailoring by Lus et Befve.

68 **Carl Erickson** 'Combien de Morceaux de Sucre?',*Gazette du Bon Ton,* 1922. Afternoon dress of velvet with lace 'à la Maréchale'. Designer not named. Erickson, an American, later became one of the foremost fashion illustrators of the 'thirties, working exclusively for *Vogue* under the pseudonym 'Eric'. His drawings, which later became looser in technique than this exmaple, epitomised elegant Parisian life in the years immediately before the Second World War and a good description of his working methods can be found in Bettina Ballard's autobiography *In My Fashion* (Secker and Warburg, 1960).

as though there had been no hiatus but with a difference which showed itself particularly in evening wear and in the use of cosmetics. The discreet make-up allowed to those who were neither actresses nor demi-mondaines was replaced in the post-war years by a lavish use of lipstick, rouge and eyeshadow which gave rise to censorious articles in the press—though the latter carried an increasing number of advertisements for exotically-named scents and cosmetics of all kinds. Evening dresses reflected the 'vamp' feeling with increasingly daring décolletages which often exposed the back to the waist with only a minimal covering for the breasts. This too gave rise to diatribes in correspondence columns against 'naked' women and the degeneracy of the age. Such an extreme exposure raised a new problem and the dancer Gabys Delys sponsored an advertisement which recommended to 'une lady décolletée' the Gillette razor by means of which 'she can always have armpits which are white and velvety'. The pre-war 'jupes-culottes' and harem-skirts reappeared and Chinese style pyjamas made their appearance as an alternative to the ornate teagowns which were still popular enough for dressmakers in London and Paris to specialise in their design and making. A curious and inexplicable quirk of fashion was that although fashionable women were showing more and more of their torsos the forehead remained as completely covered as it had been before 1914. Hats, particularly the cloche variety, came so far down over the eyes as to make their wearers almost unrecognisable; evening turbans and bandeaux served the same function—even the hair was arranged to cover most of the forehead.

69 André Marty 'La Biche Apprivoisée', *Gazette du Bon Ton,* 1922. A black and white dress with bands of ornament with sleeves and lining of the side drapery in scarlet. Designed by Paul Poiret.

The *Gazette du Bon Ton* resumed its regular publication in the same format, with the same contributors and illustrators. A newcomer was the talented Eduardo Garcia Benito, a Spaniard, who signed himself Benito. Prior to this his drawings had been reproduced in a new publication, *Les Feuillets d'Art* which had appeared in 1919. This was also published by Lucien Vogel as an expensively produced portfolio with loose sections and contents devoted to the

LE JAZZOFLUTE
ROBE DU SOIR, DE BEER

70 Georges Lepape 'Le Jazzoflute', *Gazette du Bon Ton,* 1922. Coral pink silk evening dress with bands of silver-beaded embroidery designed by Beer. The jazzoflute, a passing craze in the early 'twenties, somewhat resembled a bicycle pump in appearance; the notes were produced by adjusting the plunger section. Here the model is accompanying a dance tune played on a portable gramophone.

71 Benito 'On se reverra, j'espère . . .', *Gazette du Bon Ton,* 1922. Walking costume in black, banded with sable, by Martial et Armand and a man's overcoat in dark blue cloth by Lus et Befve. Unusual in showing male and female fashion in the same plate.

arts in general; each issue usually included one or more plates *hors-texte*, which had some reference to fashion. Drawings by Benito were a regular feature in the *Gazette du Bon Ton* from 1920 onwards and Poiret, always anxious to encourage a rising star, commissioned Benito to paint a portrait of him and Madame Poiret which was exhibited in the Salon of 1922. Of course, Benito drawings of Poiret models appeared regularly in the *Gazette*. His work and that of others was considered of such interest that they were bound together, with no text or editorials, into two volumes, each containing one hundred plates, and published under the title *Le Bon Ton d'après Guerre*. The period covered was that between 1920 and 1922.

Benito carried to extremes the distortions which are necessary in fashion illustrations to emphasise the line of a couture model, or to stress the essential personality of a dress. Most illustrators tended to attenuate the body under the dress—particularly so in the early years of the 'twenties when the majority of dresses were straight from the shoulder to the hem with the line broken only by a detail at hip level to accentuate the low waist. They also made the legs extremely slender and elongated the necks of the figures to an entirely unnatural degree. The distortion of a tiny head on a very long neck had a historical precedent, being reminiscent of the Mannerist style of painting, particularly in the work of the sixteenth-century painter, Parmigianino. A new tendency to treat the underlying female form in terms of simply treated

72 André Marty 'Laisse le moi prendre . . .', *Gazette du Bon Ton,* 1922. Evening dress and young girl's day dress designed by Jeanne Lanvin.

cylindrical forms was no doubt due to the increasing interest in Negro sculpture which had played a great part in Cubist painting before the war but which had come more to the notice of the public as a result of the Colonial Exhibition held at Marseilles in 1922. Here the sculpture and artifacts from France's numerous colonies in Equatorial Africa had awakened an interest which was to play a great part in influencing the decorative arts for the rest of the decade.

73 Benito 'Au revoir, mon amour', *Gazette du Bon Ton,* 1922. Afternoon dress by Paul Poiret. A black and white ensemble relieved only by the jade green tassel on the vanity case and the handle of the typically heavy umbrella.

74 Anonymous   Left to right: blue cashmere dress trimmed with Chinese braid and a dress of salmon pink taffeta, both by Jeanne Hallée; grey crêpe dress with multi-coloured beaded belt by Jenny; black velvet dress embroidered with silver by Paul Poiret. It was the policy of the magazine *Art, Goût et Beauté* not to mention the names of the artists contributing the illustrations which were reproduced by the pochoir process, 1923.

Fashion illustrators were in fact exploring the ground broken by Amadeo Modigliani who had died tragically in 1920. Artists such as Charles Martin, Benito, Georges Lepape, Charles Laborde and Léon Bénigni must have been aware of Modigliani's work to a greater extent than the general public and more sympathetic to his aims which began to be appreciated very soon after his death by the more perceptive. But others like Pierre Brissaud, Etienne Drian, George Barbier and André Marty eschewed such exaggeration, finding their ideas of elegance could be expressed by adhering to more normal proportions with only the slightest of adjustments.

Considering that many of these illustrators could well be alive at the time of writing, there

75 Anonymous Three models by Jeanne Lanvin, left to right: 'Nadine' a salmon-pink dress with silver embroidery; 'Marquise' dress in blue satin with a characteristic Lanvin full skirt; 'Héloïse' black crêpe embroidered in white and silver. *Art, Goût et Beauté,* 1923.

is a curious lack of information about them. Some of those illustrated in this volume, Raoul Dufy, Jean Gabriel Doumergue and Kees van Dongen are, of course, now well known as painters or portraitists and their lives are well documented. Dufy's collaboration with Poiret as a textile designer antedated his subsequent fame as a recorder of Parisian life and in the early 'twenties his work as a fashion illustrator was mainly to publicise the fabrics he still designed for the firm of Bianchini. Van Dongen painted many brilliant portraits of fashionable women which epitomised the feeling of the 'twenties and those in the Musée d'Art Moderne are too little known. Doumergue's idiosyncratic portraits of the beauties of several generations—his career continued long enough for him to paint Brigitte Bardot—invariably had the familiar distortion of the neck and he showed a partiality for the fashions of *c.* 1922 with their long bodices and very full skirts starting at a low waist line.

The 'twenties and particularly the first half of the decade, saw a remarkable activity on the part of these artists for apart from the continuing demand for their work from the *Gazette*

76 Anonymous White full skirted dress by Jeanne Lanvin with motifs of English embroidery, re-embroidered in red. Pink crêpe dress by Doucet. *Art, Goût et Beauté,* 1923.

77 Anonymous 'Plumage', a grey crêpe dress with sleeves and skirt panels of gold lace embroidered with coral by Philippe et Gaston. *Art, Goût et Beauté,* 1923.

opposite
XIV Etienne Drian Fashion drawing reproduced in *Feuillets d'Art,* 1920. The name of the couturier is not mentioned.

XV George Barbier 'Des Roses dans la Nuit.' Fashion drawing from *Gazette du Bon Ton,* 1921. Evening dress by Worth.

78 Anonymous Porcelain vase painted in orange and sepia with figures wearing furs in the fashions of 1923. Made by J. Bernardaud et Cie of Limoges for a Parisian furrier jauntily named 'A la Reine d'Angleterre'.

du Bon Ton until its demise in 1925 their drawings appeared in numerous other magazines: *Vogue, Harper's Bazaar*—which enjoyed the exclusive services of the brilliant Erté—and *Fémina*, which had shaken off its dowdy pre-war image and in the splendid Christmas number of 1920 reproduced the best talents of the day. *Les Feuillets d'Art, Le Goût du Jour, Le Journal des Dames, Jardin de Modes Nouvelles,* and *L'Illustration* were all anxious for imaginative and original fashion drawings, especially as there were few photographers, apart from one or two already under exclusive contract, capable of conveying the messages of the current styles.

There was however a decline in the amount of fashion drawing around 1925, the year when the *Gazette Du Bon Ton* merged with *Vogue* and no doubt the recurring economic crises of the 1920's were responsible for putting many of the expensively produced periodicals out of action. The success and réclame which many of the artists had gained opened up opportunities of designing for the theatre or for the rapidly expanding film industry. The chance of realising their own ideas was inevitably more attractive than drawing dresses designed by another hand, however exciting those clothes might be or how few the restrictions placed upon the imagination. An even more important factor was the mania for limited *éditions de luxe* which swept France in the 'twenties. Classics and contemporary works illustrated by the leading artists of the day, often bound in lavish, specially-designed bindings, were eagerly collected; societies of bibliophiles were founded in the cities and towns of France so that subscribers could be sure of obtaining the latest publications, numerous enough to warrant a lengthy column in the magazine *L'Amour de l'Art* each month devoted entirely to the subject. Guy Arnoux, George Barbier, Léon Bénigni, Benito, Robert Bonfils, Pierre Brissaud, Brunelleschi, Etienne Drian, Georges Lepape, Charles Martin and André Marty found a lucrative demand for contributions which brought a considerable degree of prestige. After 1925, when Art Deco, with its stress on curves and floral motifs was giving way to the Cubist-influenced, more geometrical Modernism, the new fashions, with their extremely short skirts and contrived simplicity, proved less amenable to decorative or fantastic compositions than the more elaborate fashions of the first half of the decade.

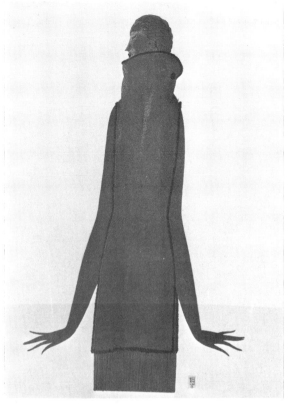

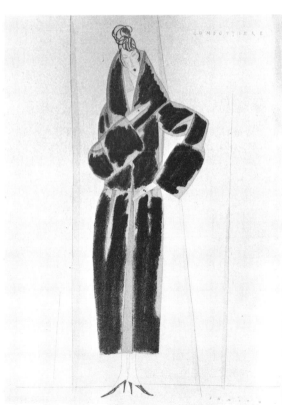

79, 80, 81 Benito Three of a series of plates lavishly printed in black, silver and gold with occasional touches of colour. They formed an album of models for the 1923 season issued under the title *La Dernière Lettre Persanne* by Fourrures Wiel.

82 **Madeleine Fabre** Porcelain figure of a girl in a black and white evening dress carrying a green fan. Possibly inspired by a model by Madeleine Vionnet exhibited in the Pavillon d'Elégance at the 1925 Paris Exhibition.

83 **Etienne Drian** Fashion drawing, c. 1925.

overleaf, page 96
84 **Reynaldo Luza** Evening dress by Chanel 1927. An illustration of the reaction against the short skirts; in this model the skirt, while still short in front, descends to ankle length at the back in a series of bias-cut frills from a low waistline.
overleaf, page 97
85 **Jean Dupas** American fashion advertisement, 1927.

Lepape, Benito and Marty continued to work for *Vogue* and *Harper's Bazaar* as did Erté and a newcomer, Reynaldo Luza, whose work had much in common with that of Erté. Jean Dupas, a mural painter whose decorative compositions had been featured in a number of the pavilions at the 1925 Paris Exhibition, was in considerable demand by advertising agencies in the United States whose accounts included a number of large department stores. The technical improvements in photography, and more importantly, in the reproduction of photographs inevitably resulted in the reduction of the number of fashion drawings: a magazine's editorial staff welcomed the freedom to compose layouts from dozens of photographs of a dress taken

Reynaldo Luza

opposite
Jean Dupas

ARNOLD CONSTABLE

COMMEMORATING THE MODE OF YESTERDAY
PRESENTING THE MODE OF TO-DAY
FORECASTING THE MODE OF TO-MORROW

86 Léon Bénigni Advertisement for Lever Brothers, 1928.

87 Reynaldo Luza Afternoon ensemble by Redfern, *Harper's Bazaar,* 1929. The dress of lime green panne velvet is intricately cut and its matching coat with elbow-length sleeves and a hemline dipping at the back is trimmed with monkey fur.

at a single sitting compared with a sketch which, however accomplished, might not please everybody. In the 'thirties colour photography reproduction was still not satisfactory; consequently the editorial pages of the few prestige fashion magazines to have survived the depression were enlivened by the accomplished colour sketches of Erik, Willaumez and Bérard, these acting as a foil to the dramatic black and white photographs of Horst, Durst or Hoyningen-Huené. Since the last war the only enduring new talent to emerge was that of René Gruau, an accomplished draughtsman whose stylish drawings, especially those for Christian Dior, carry on the tradition of elegance set by Lepape and Iribe a half century ago.

88 Reynaldo Luza Black satin hat designed by Agnès. Described as having a drooping line to harmonise with the latest dresses it indicates a new tendency to expose the forehead which had been concealed by hats since before the war.

XVI André Marty 'Le Cendre de la Cigarette.' Fashion drawing from *Gazette du Bon Ton,* 1922. Evening dress by Paul Poiret.

XVII André Marty 'Loin des Gêneurs.' Illustration to an article on motorcars and tourism. An indication of changing times: ten years earlier the easy informality shown by the bathers existed but would not have been considered worth recording. Caravans were also a recent development.

XVIII Jean Gabriel Doumergue Portrait of Madame George Owen, 1929. The sitter is wearing one of the coloured silk wigs which enjoyed a brief popularity in the 'twenties.

89 Sem 'et un bar chez le couturier à la mode,'
L'Illustration, 1929.

Les rouges
RITZ
Pour les lèvres - Pour les joues
fleurissent la femme

opposite
XIX Jean Gabriel Doumergue 'The artist and his inspiration', 1929. Doumergue remained faithful to his concept of the ideally dressed model, with long, loosely
fitting bodices and voluminous skirts falling from hip
level. This was inspired by Lanvin in the immediate post
War period.

90 Orsi Advertisement for Ritz lipsticks, 1928.

91 Jean Dupas American advertisement for furs, 1930.

92 Jean Dupas American advertisement, 1928.

93 Léon Bénigni American advertisement, 1928.

94 André Marty American advertisement, 1928.

95 André Marty American advertisement, 1928.

96 Georges Lepape Models for daywear by Lelong and Nicole Groult drawn for an American advertisement. 1928.

97 Edouard Séguy   Design for a textile from 'Samarkande', a collection of suggestions for textile or wallpapers with a 'Persian' influence derived from the Ballets Russes, 1920.